The Wisdom Journey

A Young Man's Path to Knowledge

Min. Harrell L. Henton

Contact: Min. Harrell L. Henton

4561 N.W. 33rd Court

Miami, Fl 33142

Email: thewisdomjourney@yahoo.com

Copyright © 2018 Min. Harrell L. Henton

All rights reserved. No part of this publication may be reproduced, distributed, or transmitted in any form or by any means, including photocopying, recording, digital scanning, or other electronic or mechanical methods, without the prior written permission of the publisher, except in the case of brief quotations embodies in critical reviews and certain noncommercial uses permitted by copyright law.

Dedication

To the Late Robert L. Holt Sr., a wise leader, minister, and grandfather.

Acknowledgements

Special thanks to my Heavenly Father for His Grace and Mercy that has kept me all my days.

Thanks to my family for your invaluable support, inspiration, prayers, encouragement, and continuous wisdom. To my Brownsville Church of Christ family, I love you and thank you for your prayers over this endeavor.

To my beautiful wife Kellee, my son Harrison, and my daughter Kaleah, I thank you for all of your sacrifices that you have made so that God may use me for His purpose. I love you!!

CONTENTS

Prologue	1
Preach, Stay, and Run	5
Preach the Word	7
Stay away from the money	11
Stay away from the women	17
Many are called, but Few are chosen	21
Preach the Word, Not people	27
It's not who's right, It's what's right	31
Always take the low seat until someone brings you up	37
Never be in a room counseling a Woman alone	41
Never Give up	45
Lay no hands on any man quickly	49
Always invite your wife with you	53
Always go where you said you are going	57
The Buck Stops Here	59
Don't give to be seen, be seen Giving	63
Trust in the Lord	67
Always have money to get back	71
Never counsel before you preach	75
Keep prayer in your life	79
Stop playing and serve God	83
Two people arguing will never solve anything	87
Keep money in your pocket	91
Always learn everything you can about your job	93
Expose your children to the world	97
Prayer Changes things!	101
Sometimes you have to walk alone	105
Get Some Rest	109
Teach Change, Don't Force Change	113
Be Yourself	117

Biography

Minister Harrell L. Henton has been working for the Lord for as long as he can remember. Under the guidance of his grandfather, Robert Holt Sr., he has made the grand decision to dedicate his full life to the work of the Lord and His church. Born on July 6, 1983, he is the third of four children born to Leroy and Hester Henton. He is a graduate of Miami Carol City Senior High and after finishing there, he matriculated to Florida Memorial University, where he studied Communications.

Beginning his path toward the work of the church, Harrell became a Christian, after being baptized into the body of Christ, on January 10, 1993, at the tender age of 9. From there, Harrell continued to spend time with his grandfather and mentor, Robert Holt Sr., a minister of a small, robust congregation in Miami, Florida. Harrell began to learn an abundance about the word of God, words of wisdom, and just in general learning more about becoming a man. Little did he know at the time that he was being groomed to one day take over the ministry of the Brownsville Church of Christ. In August of 2011, Harrell, was handed the torch to deliver God's word. He was installed as the full time minister of the Brownsville Church of Christ on August 22, 2011. From there, he decided to make it his mission to continue to build the Brownsville congregation as a loving and family oriented church. With the support and encouragement of his family and membership, he has begun to build this church, increasing membership, creating more programs, and strengthening the programs already in existence. As a young man leading a great church, many times it can be difficult, but Minister Henton understands that success does not come without hard work, but he knows that with God all things are possible!

Although Bro. Henton had his plate full with a full time ministry position and working a full time job outside of the ministry, he still found the time to find his help meet. He began dating the former Kellee L. Pratt in September 2008. It perhaps was a little tough over the years considering they had a long distance relationship but through God all things are possible. They made it work and three years later in December 2011, they made it official by tying the knot. Being married for seven years, Harrell and Kellee Henton have two beautiful children, Harrison and Kaleah. Harrell has his plate full to capacity. However, he is up for the challenge. Having a close relationship with the Lord and living by the Word of God, he knows that he will be blessed, no matter what the situation is. Currently, Minister Henton is a certified Chaplain, state

The Wisdom Journey

approved pre-marital/ post – marital counselor, sought after mentor and public speaker.

Bro. Henton's written encouragement happens to be one of his favorite scriptures, "Trust in the Lord with all thine heart; and lean not unto thine own understanding, in all thy ways acknowledge Him and He shall direct thy path (Proverbs 3:5-6). Remember, the race is not given to the swift or the strong, but to those that can endure until the end.

Prologue

The art of wisdom comes from the very depths of a soul that has experienced some things thereby able to decipher between hope and failure. It is my goal in this book to share some wisdom that was once shared with me by a very wise man. I can vividly recall what it was like growing up in Miami, Florida around the age of eight years old. Somewhere in my mind, I felt like I was different from everyone else or that I saw things differently from my fellow friends. I wondered even at times why did I feel this way and everyone else sees it another way. Later on in life I found out that it was an anointing, but I will discuss that in a later chapter. I grew up in Miami-Dade, Fl., specifically in a neighborhood called Myrtle Grove. I must say, I had a pretty good life and my family always got together. It could have been holidays or birthdays…..we always found a way to come together and celebrate life. I guess you can say that at the time I thought every family was like mine, getting together, loving each other, eating together, and even attending each other graduations.

As an eight year old kid, I thought that life was great, and that the feeling that I felt was special but couldn't be explained yet. Family to me was everything, and to me my family was the best. We just loved each other! Growing up in Myrtle Grove, it allowed me to learn life from a perspective that many young children at my age didn't have to learn from. For example, my mother worked in law enforcement, and she continually kept her feet on the gas with her children. She didn't want to lose any of us to the streets, prison, or even death knowing that she had seen other mothers lose children. Therefore, because of her experiences, she seemed to strive hard to keep my two sisters, and younger brother from going down the wrong road. It was evident that she had seen a lot of disappointment, hate, rage, and regret from families in the environment that she worked in over twenty years. As a result, she vicariously brought home some major frustration that was given to her children to stay focused in school and never quit. So for me, quitting was not an option and I learned to stay focused so that I could make my mom proud. On the other hand, my father, whom I called, "daddy" was the silent assassin. My father has great work ethic and he is strong in every sense of the word. I was blessed to have my father in the house, even blessed to see how he operated in marriage which would set a blueprint for me later. My father, Leroy Henton, didn't speak much, but when he spoke, we needed to listen unless we wanted him to discipline us. My father was and still is a great role model for me, and it is through him I have the mindset to work and to love people. If something happened to any of my sisters or brother, he was always there to lend a helping hand. If our car broke down, he was there. If we needed money without mom knowing, he was there. If we needed a ride somewhere, he was there. Basically, my father was the best!! Family to me was everything, and I really am thankful to God for placing me into a family that has people that love me and most importantly, love God. Although my parents guided me, it is about my grandfather that I write this book. Robert L. Holt Sr., a man that was strong as an ox, and wise as a worldly scholar. My grandfather saw something in me at an early age that I didn't even know that I had until he brought it out of me. Picture a man that has nine children, ministers to two churches, one in Fort Pierce, and one in Brownsville, FL. A man that has a wife that is often sick, members constantly fighting against him and his vision, and having to deal with his own health problems. Nevertheless, he found it necessary to mentor his grandson. This book will articulate many practical wisdoms that I have received from him, and a few that I have learned along the way. As you read this book, remember that wisdom is the principle thing, and with all of thy getting, get an understanding.

Meditation:

Proverbs 22:17 – 19 - "*Incline your ear, and hear the words of the wise, and apply your heart to my knowledge, for it will be pleasant if you keep them within you, if all of them are ready on your lips. That your trust may be in the Lord, I have made them known to you today, even to you."*

_____

_____

_____

_____

_____

_____

Preach, Stay, and Run

It is without a doubt that I would be in prison or have many children out of wedlock if it wasn't for many of my grandfather's wisdom principles. This one principle in particular has helped me to dodge many ditches that was laid before me as a man of God. He said to me, **preach the Word, stay away from the money, and stay away from the women.** Many pastors, deacons, bishops, and leaders have fallen out of position because they failed to keep these very principles. Time and time again, many men fall because they cannot control their mouth, their wallet, and/ or their pants. It is tragic that the very thing God has entrusted in the man of God to deliver, he uses to satisfy himself for temporal gain. I want to deal with each of these principles in this section to help us to understand that if we follow those words, we will be alright. We will be able to navigate through the temptations that can easily betray us if we don't take heed.

Preach the Word

My grandfather was a proponent of preaching the word. The word in this context are the words of the Bible, and rightly dividing it to the degree where it would be sound doctrine. It is unfortunate when the word of God is used to falsely lead people into misunderstanding and/or for selfish gain. As the man of God, you have to preach the word while allowing God to be glorified, Satan to be horrified, and the name of Jesus to be magnified. In 2 Timothy 4:2- 4, Paul tells Timothy, his son in the gospel, "Preach the word! Be ready in season *and* out of season. Convince, rebuke, exhort, with all longsuffering and teaching. For the time will come when they will not endure sound doctrine, but according to their own desires, *because* they have itching ears, they will heap up for themselves teachers; and they will turn *their* ears away from the truth, and be turned aside to fables". Preaching the word is essential to the lives of those that are hearers, and it affects them to the degree where they often entrust in the source of the message. It is without a doubt that by sticking to the Word, it will allow the man of God to have a church, a congregation that will be under a teaching suitable for growth. I remember a time when a young, eager preacher was at the pulpit at a neighboring church, and he was preaching about husbands loving their wives. So, my grandfather and I were in the congregation listening to the message and representing our church. As this young preacher elaborated on husbands loving their wives, he said, "Husbands need to learn how to be men, and stop allowing the wife to run all over them!" My grandfather whispered to me and said, "He may like it when she runs over him that may be what turns him on." I started to ask him what he meant, but I wanted to hear more of what this young preacher was saying. The preacher continued, "Husbands, you must love your wife, means you have to make love to her", and as he continued, my grandfather began to have a puzzled look on his face. After the service was over, my grandfather and I began to ride back home and we spoke about the sermon. I asked him, "Granddaddy, why did you have a puzzled look on your face when the preacher was preaching?" He explained, "I had a puzzled look on my face because I didn't agree with everything that the preacher said. For example, he said, "making love to your wife doesn't mean that you love your wife." In addition, "you must learn ways to make love to your wife without touching her." So as we continued our discussion home, it was then my grandfather said, there are three things that you must do to be an effective minister. You must, preach the word, stay away from the money, and stay away from the women. It was then at twelve years old that I started to understand how my grandfather was able to overcome certain pitfalls that I heard about as a child growing up in church. He condensed a lifelong rolodex of knowledge into three simplistic points to minister with longevity and success. This chapter will articulate my experiences with a wise man that took the time out to pour into me his knowledge and understanding of the Word. As a young man, I witnessed my grandfather go through trials and tribulations particularly in the church dealing with church members. Many times we make the mistake of assuming that people are godly because they portray a Christ-like image or they attend a congregation of perceived prestige. Growing up, I found that to not be the case. Around the age of twelve, as I said earlier, I developed a passion for the word of God. It seemed like God was "calling me", and that He wanted me to be a leader of people. At this age, I felt a calling, but I could not articulate exactly what it was. My grandfather must have seen something in me because he seemed to desire me to be around him more and more. Often times it became overwhelming, for example, he would ask me Bible questions, and various scenarios on how to lead. Here I am, this twelve year old kid, hanging around a sixty year old man that is speaking to me as if I am a fellow colleague. As we began to spend more time together, I started to love our conversations, and the things that I learned while I was in his company. My grandfather always said, "Preach the word", because he seemed to be a student of the word, and thought about it every day. At this time in my life, I wasn't thinking about the word, I wanted to play basketball, football, and hang with friends in my neighborhood. However, I didn't want to leave him because he always gave me knowledge, or caused me to think more. It is without a doubt that many people today miss out on the appreciation of wisdom from the ones that have witnessed the struggle of oppression and adversity. As a result of this, some of us fall into the pitfalls of disappointment, and regret. As I began to be around my grandfather, I found that he focused when he preached. He conveyed the word of God in a way that came with power and clarity which created respect whether you liked his style or not. As a young kid I gravitated towards that, and I even watched him go through the emotions in the word as he strived to encourage people to be saved. As he and I began to spend more time together, I started to watch him more, and see his study habits, continuous praying over the text, and attempt to make a practical application for the people on Sunday. Preaching the word must be held to high regard by all men, knowing that God will hold you accountable for every word that you say and teach. So as the man of God, you must always preach the word.

Stay away from the money

For the love of money is the root of all kinds of evil. Unfortunately, some people who crave money have wandered from the true faith and pierced themselves with many sorrows. Many gospel preachers today get themselves caught up in the pursuit of obtaining riches that they will do or say anything to get it. In a recent study shared in the Smart Church Advisor, 9 out of 10 pastors are underpaid. The lack of sufficient funding can possibly cause the temptation to steal from a church that may not value them. It is always a tragedy that money has broken homes, churches, relationships, and families because of greed from the very people that have been entrusted to manage it. This principle states that in order to be successful, you have to stay away from the money. Don't touch it, don't count, and don't handle it. Why? Often times, many people have preconceived notions about the pastor, minister, or even that bishop. These preconceived notions are prevalent because of the previous corrupt preachers that have taken advantage of the trusting hearts of genuine lovers of God who expect the pastor to do the right thing. This wise principle encouraging men of God to stay away from the money is vital to a pastor's longevity and it speaks to the fact that the most effective way to refute ideas of greed is to not touch the money. You can get a report about what was collected, speak to the financial team regarding the vison of the funds, or even have the ability to encourage better giving, but stay away from the money. One day, my grandfather and I were at his house and he was trying to cash a check that the church gave him for being the senior minister. Normally, I don't go with him to the bank, but this time he asked me to drive him to the bank. Now as we are riding I noticed that my grandfather had a look on his face that seemed uncertain about something, but I wasn't sure what it was. So as I get to the bank, he asked me to go in the bank with him to cash the check. Again, he seemed a little concerned about something, and as he approaches the bank clerk window, he states to the clerk, "Can I cash this check please?" As the bank teller looks in her system, and begins to prepare to cash the church check from the church, she says, "Sorry sir, but the check cannot be cashed at this time." He asked, "Why", she states, "Because the funds are not available." It was at that point that I began to understand why my grandfather looked very down. It was because he knew that there was a possibility that money wasn't available, and that there was nothing that he could have done about it. To some, they may say that he should have had access to the money, or known about the lack of funds. However, because he did not handle the money, his perspective was that he can't be blamed for the lack of funds. It is often unfortunate that many people don't appreciate the man of God that labors among them, or the one that is there for them when they needed him the most. According to a study on Gospel Coalition online, pastors are more prone to commit suicide than any other job field in the world. Consider this thought, as a pastor, you have to be everything to everyone but it seems like no one is anything to you.

Money has always been a driving force in many individuals' ideas or opinions on what career that they want to pursue. For example, many young men grow up with the mindset to be in the NFL one day. To have the ability financially to one day support their loved ones so that they no longer have to worry about money is a driving force. It is often a young man's dream to play professionally so that he can have a big house, nice vehicle, and eat at the best restaurants. Would you say that he loves football? I would say, "Maybe", but the main drive is the accumulation of money. So money is like a two edge sword. If properly managed, money can be a great benefit to the one that has earned it. On the other hand, it can be a great danger because it will cause people to kill, lie, cheat, and even manipulate their way to the top. Therefore, as a pastor, I believe my grandfather understood that people cannot control their emotions or possess the ability to say "no" regarding temptations.

As a pastor, we should know the darkness that abides in regards to temptations that are so easily attainable with money. So the wise words that are best to heed are to, "stay away from the money" so that your good cannot be evil spoken of.

It is important to know that as minister working with a congregation, we must appreciate the man of God, and help him to be as focused on the word without distraction. According to one minister, he feels as though he cannot preach effectively because he finds himself doing all of the work. This is a major issue! Yes, I said issue because the word demands focus and meditation. Therefore, if the man of God is not able to focus and meditate on the word of God because he is concentrating on the things other should be able to manage, his focus is limited.

Meditation:

Ephesians 1: 16 – 19 - " Do not cease to give thanks for you, remembering you in my prayers, that the God of our Lord Jesus Christ, the Father of glory, may give you a spirit of wisdom and of revelation in the knowledge of him, having the eyes of your hearts enlightened, that you may know what is the hope to which he has called you, what are the riches of his glorious inheritance in the saints, and what is the immeasurable greatness of his power toward us who believe, according to the working of his great might."

_____

_____

_____

_____

_____

_____

Stay away from the women

Proverbs 5:3 states, "For the lips of the adulterous woman drip honey, and her speech is smoother than oil." There is a unique danger for the pastor when it comes to women. He must be aware of the potential scrutiny and embarrassment that comes when he decides to be involved with a woman, whether in or out the church. So what is the big deal about women whereas the man of God needs to be careful around them? First, God has given the man of God a position that is the greatest position that anyone can hold, a proclaimer of His word. Therefore, with great responsibility will come great expectations which can be very difficult for some men to handle. Also, it is very important to know that the position brings an overwhelming amount of attention, both good and bad. People are encouraged by you Oh, man of God, and they are thankful for your sacrifice to be a vessel for God. You are celebrated, respected by many, honored by your fellow laborers, and you have the words that pertain to eternal life. Oh, man of God, you have a great duty, but Satan desires to have you, he wants to sift you as wheat.

It is very important to know that your life is celebrated, as a result, and there are some women that are seeking to show their appreciation to you. My grandfather told me that I can make it as a minister if I learn how to control my flesh and be able to discern the motives of those that are in my life. God created the woman to be an important part in a man's life. It has been difficult for man from the beginning as we see in the book of Genesis. As Eve began to be tempted by the serpent, the serpent continued to speak to her in an attempt to possibly get to man. Eve listened to the trickery words of the serpent, partook of the fruit, and then gave it to her husband, Adam. Adam was made in the image of God, but he didn't have the desire to make the right decision so that he could continue to abide in the Garden of Eden. Men today sometimes struggle with their ability to resist the power of a woman. The advice that I was given as a young man is that women are good but be careful. For example, when I was about nineteen years old, I began to like girls, and some of them liked me. At this time in my life, I was in college, just starting to preach, and it seemed like my attraction for women became stronger. For me, this feeling was able to stay under control, but I always felt it in the deepest of my spirit that I wanted to be with a lady. Therefore, I attempted things so that I could gain creditability so that I could have conversations with my fellow peers. As a young preacher, I found that temptation began to get greater the more that I got into the Lord and His church. My grandfather spoke with me during these times, and he guided me with the words that helped me to not fall into pre-marital sex, having a baby out of wedlock, or even contracting a detrimental disease. This book is being written because the danger that a lot of young men face is the inability to say, "No", and to keep moving forward. Satan knows that you have a calling on your life to preach, sing, encourage, pray, and to be a servant in God's Kingdom. When I was about twenty one years old, I was faced with the challenge of my life, and I believe if I would have given into this challenge, I wouldn't be a minister today. It was a regular day, and I received a call from one of the members of the church where I was serving at the time. On the other side of the phone was a wiling sister that was ready to please me in any way possible. She stated that she wanted to be with me in a way that is reserved for married couples, although she was married herself. As a young preacher, this was obviously a satanic device attempting to lure me into a situation that could be damaging to my reputation and ministry. At the time I didn't know the severity of what could have been, but thank God my grandfather gave me this wisdom nugget to avoid this woman. On the phone, I ended up saying "no" to this woman, and even though she came to worship a few times, I never mentioned it to anyone until now. Temptation comes in many forms and fashions and the Bible tells us simply in James 4:7, "Submit yourselves therefore to God. Resist the devil, and he will flee from you." Satan attempts to come through women that often times are attractive and willing to go as far as you let them. Oh man of God, stay away from the women, and keep praying that your faith don't fail. When you see yourself about to fall, pray. When you find yourself in a precarious situation, resist the devil. Stay away from the women!

Meditation:

Proverbs 19:20 "Hear counsel, and receive instruction, that thou mayest be wise in thy latter end."

_____

_____

_____

_____

_____

_____

Many are called, but Few are chosen

Growing up in a home full of church goers can be difficult. It is like the feeling you get when you find yourself in the midst of perfection, but not being able to measure up. My family has been in the body of Christ for a long time. Their faith dates back to the early 50's which begun with my great grandfather, Granddaddy Buster whom was a member of Hallandale Beach church of Christ. As a result of his faithfulness, the backbone of our family started with God. As a result of Granddaddy Buster's faith and his strong values, our family had an intense love for God and this love has always been the driving force of our lifestyle, our dress, our language and the way that the children in our family are raised. Fast forward to July 1983, I was born at North Miami Hospital to the parents of Leroy and Hester Henton. It is without a doubt that this was a great day, and that God was smiling from heaven displaying all of His glory. Not really, but it was a good day! As a little boy, I have always felt the feeling that I am a little different from everyone in this world. It seemed like God had always had His hand on me and that one day I would be used as a vessel for His glory. I remember in first grade at Myrtle Grove Elementary in Miami Gardens, FL, I had my first encounter with a greater power, which is God. One day, as I am walking through the halls going from one classroom to another, I see kids running pass me to see a fight that was occurring. As I began to start running with them, there was something inside of me saying, "You need to go to class, and not this fight." My immediate response was, "Who the heck is talking to me?" I didn't understand this inner voice, or that I may have a conscience. For a seven year old boy, I was totally confused, but I followed the instructions of this strange voice and I went to class. I believe this was the beginning of me hearing the voice of God. Many times we ignore the signs, and voices that try to steer us in the right direction, as a result, we find ourselves in circumstances that become very difficult to overcome. I believe that I made the right decision to avoid the fight that was going on, and it allowed me to be in the right place, whereas, others that were just bystanders began to feed the spirit at this early age of hate, and watching another person get b eat up unjustly. The Bible says in Obadiah 1:12; "You should not gloat over your brother in the day of his misfortune, nor rejoice over the people of Judah in the day of their destruction, nor boast so much in the day of their trouble." In retrospect, I believe this was the reason this "voice" was in me to help me to understand principles that will assist me as I grow older. Throughout my adolescent days, I felt different from others, and I was always pulled to go a total different direction. Therefore, I didn't always hang with my peers, it seemed as though I didn't fit in because something was calling me to obtain wisdom, knowledge, and understanding. So as I grew up, I began to be drawn to my grandfather, Robert L. Holt Sr. because he seemed to have a wisdom that my spirt desired to obtain. I watched him every time I had a chance to find out his flaws and inconsistencies. However, to my surprise, he was the same person at home that he was in the pulpit. Therefore, I began to hang out with him, and spend a lot of time with him through my boyish years up to my teenage years. The question that people ask me is, "Did you know that you were going to be a preacher?" My answer to them is, "no", but I knew that I was different from others in my circle. At the age of fifteen, I preached my very first sermon, "Fish of the Church". It was a sermonette, which mean it lasted for about five minutes, but it gave me a feeling that I never felt before. While preaching, it seemed like I was where I needed to be and that I was on top of the world. What is your calling? What makes you happy? Are you living, or are you alive? As a little boy, I was surrounded by righteousness, but I made a choice to follow the path that is seldom chosen in such a youthful stage, the godly path. At the age of twelve, I began to really get into the word of God, and desire the pure milk of God. One Sunday morning, my grandfather preached a message entitled, "Move the clay out the way", meaning get rid of all the excuses. My friend and I had been talking about being baptized, but we were a little afraid. So on this Sunday, I told him, if he goes up to be baptized, I will go up too. When my grandfather said at the end of his sermon, "if you are ready to be baptized, come on up", my friend began to walk. Here I at am twelve years old about to make a serious decision that was going to change my whole life. As soon as he walked up, I started to follow directly behind him. On this day, I was baptized for the remission of my sins, and I felt God speaking to my spirit saying, "I called you when you were in your mother's womb." This was a great day, and I remember my family being so happy for me and my new journey in life. It is without a doubt that I am called to preach, teach, and minster to the people that are in need of healing and restoration. All of us must walk in our calling, and accept it because it is the thing that God has placed us on this earth to do. After being baptized, I started to study the word of God more, go to revivals, attend gospel meetings, follow preachers, and even try to be like them. I wasn't called to be a firefighter, police officer, or president of the United States, but I was called to be a man of God. With that calling comes the responsibility to commune with God daily and to allow Him to speak to your spirit so that you can give His people a Word.

Meditation:

Psalm 19:7 - "The law of the LORD is perfect, restoring the soul; The testimony of the LORD is sure, making wise the simple."

_____

_____

_____

_____

_____

_____

Preach the Word, Not people

What is your greatest fear? My fear is that people will try to take advantage of me, and attempt to use my meekness as a weakness. It has been my experience that "church hurt" is a pain that often times is very difficult to overcome. It is difficult because the very people that are depended on to treat you right, or love you may be the ones that hurt you the most. Oh young man, you have a powerful platform as a man of God. You possess the ability to hold the attention of your members and at times it may be tempting to use that influence to preach on your personal pain. A word of caution….. Don't do it! Some "church folk" are going to cause you grief or even sorrow because people often make simple things complex. As a minister, God speaks to you so that you can speak to His children, but the natural man inside of you sometimes wants to come out and just tell "church folk" about themselves. You must resist this temptation, you must not allow yourself to succumb to the desires of your heart, and you must allow your spirit to be connected to God's Spirit. It is God's

Spirit that will direct you to preach His Word, not His children. You need to make sure that God is your guide, and that He shows you the way as you strive to let Him be glorified through your words, speech, and conversation. This chapter speaks to the one that has to battle the desire to hurt, belittle, and to rebuttal everyone that comes at you the wrong way. As a human, we have a reaction that sometimes results in us hurting first and dealing with the consequences later. As a result, you can find yourself in a world of trouble and it may become very difficult to get out of the chaos that you caused because you couldn't hold your tongue. As a person that is depended upon to make the right decisions all the time, you must always be self-aware and be careful what you say before you say it. Therefore, as you prepare to study then deliver God's words to the people, you must pray that your spirit is guided by God and not the pain someone causes you. As a wise man once said to me, "God has allowed you to have the mic, so act right." My grandfather told me as a young man striving to be better and preach God's words, "preach the word, and not people!" At the time of him telling me these things, I didn't understand what he was trying to tell me or even prevent me from doing. However, as the days and years continued, I began to realize that sometimes you will have the feeling to misuse the position and pulpit that God has allowed you to have to speak "your mind" instead of speaking God's words. Growing up in the church, people would sometimes be condescending towards me and my family. As a teenager, I preached a sermon one Sunday entitled, "Sleeping in the wrong women's lap" which focused on abstaining from bad relationships. In this sermon I spoke from the book of Judges Chapter 16 which highlighted the story of Samson and Delilah. At the end of worship, I stood in the back to shake hands, and I remember one particular person whispered in my ear, "What do you know about women, you are just a virgin!" This was crazy to hear because I never would have imagined anyone in the church to say something so offensive or even so assuming. My reaction to this was a brief blank stare which ended with a smile and a brief laugh. Throughout that whole week, I was thinking about this person, and their comment. Yes, I was a virgin, but how could you gain the courage to step to me in that manner. I started working on a sermon driven by hate, and frustration, and I was going to title it, "Get the hell out of here." This sermon was going to focus on not allowing the devil to use you which is correct, but it was focused on a person not God's people. I was driven by my anger, and I was going to use the pulpit to tell that person off by using scripture. Needless to say, I spoke with my grandfather about it before I preached it, and he strongly recommended that I don't… I didn't. He knew that anger was my driving force, and he always tried his best to prevent me from making bad decisions. My grandfather said that I have to always remember that everyone will not like or respect you, but don't allow their dislike to flow into your spirit thereby making you display the same characteristics. As you go through life young man, remember, preach the Word not people.

Meditation:

1 Corinthians 12:8 - "For to one is given the word of wisdom through the Spirit, and to another the word of knowledge according to the same Spirit;"

It's not who's right, It's what's right

Right is right and wrong is wrong! This concept of "doing the right thing" is sometimes overlooked for the pursuit of money, happiness, love, family, and even sex. It is without a doubt that all of us have chosen to do things that we know were not right and because of that, we reaped what we sowed. Similarly, we have all made bad decisions based upon what we thought was the right thing to do even though it wasn't what we wanted to do. As a young man, I was raised to seek God for the right path and to pray about what you should do. This thought process was always continual in my house to the point where I didn't look at any other way to figure out problems. This is not a bad thing. Sometimes you can hear something so much that you start to believe it. My perception began to be very godly and at an early age I made Him my primary focus. As a result, I began to look to God regarding every decision that I made for the most part. Everyone wasn't brought up the way that I was and because of that, many people have found themselves making bad choices. While growing up and traveling with my grandfather, I had an opportunity to see the differences between how people would behave in public and private. There was a time when my grandfather was speaking with a member at the church and he allowed me to be in the meeting to learn. Because of God's grace, I learned something truly meaningful that day. As my grandfather was talking to this member, he seemed very aggravated and upset because this person seemed to have been causing problems in the church. At the time I did not know what it was about but that day I learned that being a minister is much more than just preaching. As the conversation continued, my grandfather simply told this member, "I don't want to have to withdraw from you but I will." He was saying this because this member had spread rumors about a few people in the church thereby causing turmoil amongst members and leadership. It had become very confusing for me because this person was someone I thought was my grandfather's friend, and buddy. However, my grandfather dealt with this member solely in a biblical sense and not as someone he shared a longstanding friendship. He stated to me later that you cannot allow favoritism to take a hold in your ministry because people will then want to do what they want to do. My mindset that day was totally blown because he rebuked his friend, and I never thought that I would see that happen. My grandfather was a peaceful, loving, patient, and faithful person.

He always tried to help those in need. Nevertheless, he was not hesitant to rebuke a person, even his friend(s). Later that evening, my grandfather asked me to come by his house so he could speak with me. When I arrived to his house, he said, "Bro. Henton, it's not who's right, it's what's right." As he said this to me, he looked me in my eyes, and I saw the burden of ministering etched in his eyes. He wanted me to know that you have to learn how to stand up straight and not be afraid to speak to a person directly. In addition, he said, "there is going to come a time when I will not be here, and I want God to tell me, well done!" As we spoke that night until about 1am in the morning he explained to me how he was forced to nearly withdraw from one of his own friends. When you minister or even lead a team, you must do so without favoritism. When leading the church, you must make decisions based upon biblical knowledge and God's guidance. The Bible has ample guidance for church leaders to make decisions and concrete examples on how to lead your church to be great. A church is full of many personalities. Although some are structured differently, all of them should be guided by God's Words. By following the word of God, you will begin to remove the idea that it is your decision and begin to realize your decisions are guided by God's words. It is never easy to rebuke, but the apostle Paul says in **2 Timothy 4:2; Preach the word; be instant in season, out of season; reprove, rebuke, exhort with all**

longsuffering and doctrine (KJV). As the angel of the house, there will be times that you must reprimand, express sharp disapproval because of a person's behavior, and strongly encourage someone to do something. When I was given the blessed opportunity to lead God's people and teach them His Word, my grandfather had just become the minister emeritus. As he began to step back and began to hold my hand up, he said, "if I get out of line, don't be afraid to rebuke me sharply." This was amazing because at this time he still had the ability to still strongly influence of the people while gradually stepping down as senior minister. Nevertheless, he wanted me to know that as I lead God's people, no one is exempt from correction, and if I am to be effective, I cannot choose whom I have to reprimand sharply. O man of God, you have a responsibility to lead God's people to a higher mark knowing that it will not be comfortable, but it will be right in God's sight. Remember, it's not who's right, it's what's right. Lead without fear!!

Meditation:

2 Chronicles 1:10 - *"Give me now wisdom and knowledge, that I may go out and come in before this people, for who can rule this great people of Yours?"*

_____

_____

_____

_____

_____

_____

Always take the low seat until someone brings you up

The Bible reads in Luke 14:8, "when someone invites you to a wedding feast, do not take the place of honor, for a person more distinguished than you may have been invited". This scripture is an appropriate one to live by as one begins to gain prestige. As men of God, we believe that we are very important and that we should be respected. Therefore, we are hopeful that people recognize our position and prestige in God. Scripture speaks about the man of God being a vessel for God and God's Spirit working through him so that he may be used for His Glory. While leading there may be times when you feel as though you need to be recognized. Let's face it, most of us would like to be recognized in a positive way. I learned this thought process very early as a young man. I noticed that my grandfather always approached things with a humble mentality. He would sometimes be very discreet when he went to visit churches and various events in the community. He took the biblical approach of taking the low seat until someone brought him up to a more distinguished seat. Arrogance shouldn't be a part of the spirit of a man of God because God doesn't bless arrogance. Scripture says in Psalms 37, "Fret not yourself because evil doers, neither be envious of the workers of iniquity...". Taking the low seat is the mindset that says that we must be humble in our approach and learn not to assume we are always appreciated. Therefore, when we are invited to an event, we must be aware that we shouldn't assume we are the most important person in the audience... in actuality, we may not be. My grandfather stated to me that in order to be appreciated, you must have the Christian characteristic of humility. Even though God has anointed you to be the man of God/ woman of God, you must always approach His Grace with a low degree mind. My grandfather practiced this so much that it seemed to me that he was not respected as much as I believed he should have been because he wasn't a part of "special group of ministers". I feel like my grandfather is in the middle, whereas, he was open to socializing but he was often overlooked. As a result, he seldom received invites to preach, he wasn't always recognized as being in the midst, and he never was appreciated to the degree I believe that he should have been. So the question is, are you humble enough to be overlooked? Do you seek to be acknowledged because of your position, or your spirit? Do you make people place you on a pedestal, or do you wait for God to do that? O young man of God, sometimes people will not give you the respect that you desire or believe that you deserve, but stay humble! It can become frustrating knowing that God has ordained you to lead His people, but you are not always respected that way. Therefore, you must always humble yourself in God's sight, and in due time he will lift you up. Always take the low seat until someone brings you up. Humility brings room for hope and it teaches you to give God the glory for any advancements.

Meditation:

Proverbs 4: 5-9 **–** "Get wisdom, get understanding; do not forget my words or turn away from them. Do not forsake wisdom, and *she* will protect you; love her, and she will watch over you. The beginning of wisdom is this: Get wisdom. Though it cost all you have, get understanding. Cherish her, and she will exalt you; embrace her, and she will honor you. She will give you a garland to grace your head and present you with a glorious crown."

_____

_____

_____

_____

_____

_____

Never be in a room counseling a Woman alone

As a young man I would ponder was it really wrong to counsel a woman alone. We both have the spirit of God, and we both are trying to solve a problem that has been placed before us. As a young man, I wasn't aware that "church" women sometimes have ulterior motives and seek opportunities to take advantage of a person of stature or position. My grandfather shared with me that when you counsel women, never do it alone. The reason behind this is because he had witnessed many men fall from their positions because they failed to take adequate precaution. As men we can sometimes be naïve. Many of us believe that we cannot be tempted or that a woman will not come on to us. Recent events around the country has allowed us to witness the ripple effect of how men are being accused of and face significant consequences for sexual misconduct. The numbers are increasing rapidly to the extent that many people such as senators, entertainers, movie executives, and even talk show hosts are being dismissed from their position of influence. Sexual misconduct or abuse will soon come knocking at the doors of the church. It is without a doubt that sexual misconduct goes on in the church assembly. Often times it is overlooked or ignored but it does happen. This is not to say that sexual misconduct happens at the church intentionally, but it can be perceived as if it is because of the love we strive to have one towards another. Consider the brother in Christ that expresses his "love" for the sister that is dealing with bereavement. Think about the brother that makes sure he compliments sisters when they are wearing a nice dress, have beautiful skin, or those who lose weight. In the church setting these type of things can be laughed away and even ignored. We so freely demonstrate love for one another that others who are new to the faith or visit our congregations may not enjoy the display of "love" that we often demonstrate toward one another. Therefore, you must be careful that you do not counsel any women alone. First, she is coming to you for counseling because she's dealing with some things. Second, she may be in a vulnerable state, and as her counselor, you may not know where her vulnerability lies which can be sexual. Last, you must recognize that there are some women in the church that are admirers of you and they will attempt to seize opportunities to entrap you because they want to be your woman, or "side chick". My grandfather explained to me one day and he said to me very plainly,

"Son, everyone is not godly although they may appear to be". When he said this, he continued to speak about the various men that we know of that at some point were naïve and as a result, they lost their ministry. In some instances, these men also lost their family. To ensure there is no hint of impropriety, ensure that when you counsel a woman that you have another faithful sister in the room with you, preferably a seasoned saint. This approach will likely provide comfort for the sister that you are counseling and provide security for you as the counselor. Also, explain to the woman that has come in for counseling that you have the senior sister in the room to prevent any misconceptions that could arise because of the negative thinking of members. It should always be your intention to protect the flock even sometimes from themselves. If the senior sister cannot accommodate your need for her to be there, you could request for the woman to reschedule, or if it seems to be an emergency, provide counsel over the telephone. Again, you must strive to allow your spirit to be used so that your flesh is not driving you to commit an iniquity against God's Word. The thought behind this is, never place yourself in a circumstance that isn't aligned with good wisdom. Therefore, heed the words of this principle, and keep it close to your heart so that you will forever have a name that is respectable.

Meditation:

Ecclesiastes 7:12 - "For wisdom is a defense as money is a defense, But the excellence of knowledge is that wisdom gives life to those who have it."

_____

_____

_____

_____

_____

_____

Never Give up

The worse thing that anyone can do is give up when times get tough. It is said that "when the going gets tough, the tough gets going." This is very interesting because it means that when times seem to be challenging we must not allow ourselves to succumb to the pressures of that situation. Therefore, as we look at this wisdom principle, it seeks to encourage to keep pressing forward by faith no matter the situation. My grandfather stated to me that he wanted to give up on preaching and even being in ministry because it was always challenging him. Imagine trying to lead a group of people from a plethora of places, attitudes, mindsets, and even cultures to achieve a common goal. This can be challenging! When you have a vision from God and it seems that it is always being challenged and opposed as a leader you may contemplate giving up. As a man of God, quiet as it is kept, sometimes you begin to wonder why I am doing this. Sometimes the pay is not what it should be, it seems like no one wants to work together, and there will be times when your personal life seems to have its ups and downs. Nevertheless, never give up! As you begin to feel the desire to give up, remember that God is with you and that He is able to keep you strong in the midst of struggle. This wisdom is oftentimes overlooked because as millennials enter into the workplace, we see that there are so many options. We have tons of career, relationship, and even churches to minister to options that we don't have a problem with just leaving. Our mindset is that we can find another one "in a minute". We have been conditioned because of the ability to get something, anything in a matter of seconds that there is no reason to wait or even learn to be patient in the midst of a storm. My grandfather drove one hundred miles every Sunday from Miami, FL to Fort Pierce, FL to preach to a church at that time that sometimes compensated him along with his eight children with fish and fruits. Imagine someone giving you fish and fruit for you labor in these days and times. Many of us would be ready to leave that congregation because they are not on the level that we think they need to be on. In the midst of such disrespect and humiliation, my grandfather accepted these things without giving up on God and without allowing the present to affect his hope for the future. My favorite scripture to lean on when I want to give up is Proverbs 3: 5 – 6, "Trust in the Lord with all your heart, and lean not to your own understanding, but in all your ways acknowledge Him, and He (God) will direct your paths." We may tend to lean to our own understanding when things seems uncertain, but never give up! When my grandfather told me this, he wasn't saying allow people to take advantage of you, but his thought was to not be so quick to quit because things aren't going the way that you anticipated them to go. In your life you cannot develop a mindset of giving up because you then develop a habit of giving up. This creates within you the inability to stay strong. Biblically, it states in Second Chronicles 15:7, "But as for you, be strong and do not give up, for your work will be rewarded (NIV)." It is always easier to give up than to go through the process of making it and many people do not want to go "through" it. Remember, never give up and always hold on to God's unchanging hand!

Meditation:

Proverbs 3: 5 – 6 - "Trust in the LORD with all your heart and lean not on your own understanding; in all your ways submit to him, and he will make your paths straight."

_____

_____

_____

_____

_____

_____

Lay no hands on any man quickly

Scripture tells us in First Timothy 5:22 that we should not lay hands suddenly on no man, neither be partaker of other men's sins; keep thyself pure. Sometimes when you feel like there is a need, you want to place people in position to fulfill a particular need to ensure the work can be done. However, this is not the best thing to do. Many men and women are not living right. They sometimes desire position but their current condition makes them unfit to serve in the moment. Therefore, you must be careful of appointing people without prayer and supplication. As the leader of God's flock, you have to be wise in your decisions and not allow emotions, intimidation, need, or money influence your decision to ordain anyone. Statistics from the Pew Research Center verifies that there are more women in the church than there are men. As a result, sometimes you put men in places that they may be "able" to perform the task, but they are not "faithful" in their service to God or even His kingdom. As the man of God, you may have to walk alone until God sends laborers into the vineyard, church, and your business. God has strengthened you, oh man of God, to be able to handle business until those that He desire to serve are able and faithful. Growing up, I saw many men and women assume positions that they felt that they were ready for, but they weren't. So when criticism, trouble, and even loneliness set in, there was a desire to quit and no longer serve. They wanted to be in the perceived spotlight, but they weren't ready for the heat that came under those lights. My grandfather sometimes had to sing, pray, preach, facilitate the Lord's Supper, and count the offering because many men and women weren't ready to serve consistently. As a result, he leaned on this thought process. Although he was doing the majority of the work, the church moved forward. When I was around fourteen years old, I heard a few men ask my grandfather to preach, become an elder, serve as a deacon, yet they rebelled his leadership. These men did not want to be told what to do or given any advice which was given in love because in their mind they wanted to be seen, but yet they didn't want to hear. One night, my grandfather took me to his house to talk with me about the politics of the church. He stated, "I am praying for faithful brethren, and I want to appoint leaders, however they are nowhere to be found when it is time to receive teaching. " He relayed to me that he must be very careful to just appoint men and women to be leaders in church because it could potentially cause division in the church because you all are leading in different directions. Man of God, I know sometimes it gets hard to lead by yourself and that you don't want to do **EVERYTHING** by yourself, but God is your strength. Be careful being quick to appoint men and women into positions knowing that they may be able to perform it, but they are not faithful to God's Kingdom. Biblically, Moses' father- in- law, Jethro, comes to visit Moses after God delivered the children of Israel from bondage. Seeing the burden that Moses has, he tells him, "you are doing too much". In due time, Moses takes him time to appoint helpers to lighten his responsibilities. Lay no hands on any man quickly and don't be so easily persuaded by people, for God is your supervisor.

Meditation:

Proverbs 17:27 -28 - "The one who has knowledge uses words with restraint, and whoever has understanding is even-tempered. Even fools are thought wise if they keep silent, and discerning if they hold their tongues."

_____

_____

_____

_____

_____

_____

Always invite your wife with you

My grandfather was married for over thirty years and he had a lovely wife that loved him and God. She always had a smile on her face, and she always looked for the good in everyone. So when my grandfather told me this, I was skeptical of its meaning because I wasn't married at this time. He understood the difficulties of being a minister of a church that had serious demands with very little help. However, he stated to me that it is imperative that you invite your wife with you EVERYWHERE you go. As a young man, I wondered why I would want to do that. She may not be invited the places that I am invited to. However, he further explained, your wife is your advocate, she is your friend, and she is your helpmate. She sometimes has to sit in the midst of the congregation as people are talking about you and will hear things that clearly let her know that some people don't appreciate you. In the midst of that, she still has to smile, encourage, and pray for all the people where her husband has been invited to preach. Furthermore, my grandfather said inviting your wife will allow her to know that you appreciate her company, more so, it allows her to make the decision if she wants to go with you or not. Your wife watches sometimes as other "sisters in Christ" attempt to get a cheek kiss from you or a big hug from their favorite preacher. She stands strong without losing faith in the knowledge that you still love her. So when you have been invited to a gathering or a speaking event, don't leave her, invite her! By doing this, you will help protect your unbalanced flesh, cease her from worrying what time you will be home, possibly prevent other women from trying to take advantage of her absence, and to you have an advocate in the audience. Many men are always on the move and we sometimes think that our wife doesn't want to go, but still invite her. As my grandfather told me this, he shared with me that he invites my grandmother everywhere because he knows that she desires to know he still wants him by his side. As a young man, I begin to understand what he was saying because as the minister, Satan is always after you. So my question to my grandfather was, when did he start doing this? His answer to me was so profound to me, he stated, "when I begin to start caring about my wife's feelings." This spoke to me because I went with him to many church gospel meetings and revivals and a good number of preachers didn't always come with their wives. I begin to question the closeness of the preacher and his bride, and as a preacher do we really invite our wives to every event? Are we protecting her from something or are we trying to free ourselves for something? As a young man of God, remember that you must always consider your wife and always show here that you are encouraged by her presence because she is your helper.

Meditation:

Proverbs 2:6 - "For the Lord gives wisdom; from his mouth come knowledge and understanding."

_____

_____

_____

_____

_____

_____

Always go where you said you are going

As a preacher, there will be times you get extremely busy because of the demand for your services. People will need you to counsel them, pray for them, visit them when they are sick, hold their newborn baby, and listen to them speak about their problems. Knowing this, it can become very complicated with your schedule and can cause you to miss out on other opportunities. Knowing this, you must always try to go where you said you are going. Although this may sound like common sense and seems obvious that we should go where we said we are going, often we just don't do it. As men of God we don't always want folks to do know where we are and what we're doing. Men of God value privacy as well. However, it is important to let someone you trust know what you're doing to ensure your safety and to hold you accountable for what you say you're going to do. Integrity as a man of God is so vital because it allows the person that holds you to a certain standard to develop trust and confidence that you are truthful. God desires for us to be truthful and honest, not attempting to be deceiving because we do not want those whom are close to us to be in our business. My grandfather always told me that as a man of God, whether you like it or not, people hold you to a standard of excellence. Therefore, it is without a doubt that being a person of transparency may allow others to have the ability to lift the burden off your shoulders, thus allowing you to be better balanced. This principle is true with everyday life because it creates a relationship where one can be trusted, people are honest, and the expectations are attainable.

Meditation:

James 3:17 - "But the wisdom that is from above is first pure, then peaceable, gentle, and easy to be in treated, full of mercy and good fruits, without partiality, and without hypocrisy."

_____

_____

_____

_____

_____

_____

The Buck Stops Here

Everyone is not to blame for problems that may arise your congregation/ business, but someone must be responsible for whatever is happening at the congregation/ business. Based on this knowledge, we have to make sure that someone takes the lead. Being a leader is not always well received. There are times when you have to make the hard choices and tough decisions. While leading others you will find yourself at times on the mountain top of celebration and being recognized as a great visionary. Similarly, there will be times when the same people will condemn you and push you aside because you are not leading the "correct" way. No matter the situation, there has to be someone who possesses the strength to address the tough questions and problems guided by wisdom. Growing up I realized that good leaders were able to handle problems and they prepared their team to handle problems as well. Biblically, we understand that Jesus Christ came to this world to die on the cross for the sins of mankind. Jesus came to pay a ransom that we were not able to pay, therefore, He gave His life. Nevertheless, throughout His life, we see that He was very disciplined and focused on the goal at hand. Jesus, although compassionate and understanding, knew that He was the main person that had to stop any foolishness that may arise within the disciples. As a leader, elder, or senior minister of a church, you must understand that someone has to have the final say. If not, the problem or circumstance will linger long enough to become a situation that is overwhelming and can cause division amongst the people. My grandfather told me that he sometimes had to make tough decisions in regards to people acting disruptive, disrespectful to one another, and even belligerent towards him because of a variety of reasons. He told me that he had to let people know that God's word rules, but God requires the man of God to enforce the responsibility as a leader. O Young man, you must understand that you will encounter obstacles that seem to be daunting, but you have to stand strong because you are the gatekeeper. It is said that respect is earned not given. Sometimes as a leader you have to demand respect even after "earning "it. When you are placed in a position to lead men and/ or women, you must understand that you will face some egos, unwanted attitudes, and even some resistance to your leadership primarily because some people don't want to be told how to do something. At an early age my grandfather started taking me to all the meetings at church as well as the ministers' meetings in the local area and I was able to witness with my own eyes how even leaders disrespect one another.

As a little child observing this, initially I didn't fully understand what was going on, but as my grandfather explained it to me, I gained more insight. For example, when I attended a meeting that was attended by ministers, elders, and deacons, it was my expectation that these men were the best fit to understand rebellious members and individuals that don't listen. However, I quickly learned that there was a reason why their congregants were the way they were because the leader conducted themselves the same way. In this meeting, these men couldn't get a thing accomplished. Everyone wanted things to go their way, and no one agreed on the most mundane of things such as when could the next meeting be held. To me, this was disappointing but yet educational because I learned two things that day: Men are stubborn and someone has to have the final say. O young man, you must be able to lead with power and humility. Remember, God positioned you in that place, business, or company to be fearless. My grandfather was a very strong man but as I grew up around him, I quickly learned that he was also a patient, understanding, honest, loving, and a humble man. The buck, meaning the responsibility, has to stop at some point in any structure or business. The shepherd leads the sheep, the CEO oversees the company, the head chef runs the kitchen, and the father is the head of the house. O young man, stand in the capacity God has placed you in. Throughout scripture, you will find examples of discipline and the ability to handle adversity. Though at times it is not easy, you must be ready to lead verbally, non-verbally, and even by power. May God bless and strengthen you as a leader!

Meditation:

Proverbs 3:7 - "Be not wise in thine own eyes: fear the LORD, and depart from evil."

_____

_____

_____

_____

_____

_____

Don't give to be seen, be seen Giving

I spoke with a young man the other day that doesn't believe in giving. He expressed to me that he wants to lead, but he is not a giver. In my mind, this is preposterous and utterly absurd. How can you lead if you are not willing to give anything to anyone? In most churches they take up an offering for various reasons. Most of the time we are encouraged to give as God has prospered in our hearts to give. Giving seems to be a cycle that is never ending. Biblically in Luke 6:38, the Bible states, "Give, and it shall be given unto you; good measure, pressed down, and shaken together, and running over, shall men give into your bosom. For with the same measure that you mete withal it shall be measured to you again." When we give out our time, talent, and our treasure, it creates a ripple effect of blessings that will be multiplied. As a leader, you must know that people are watching you and sometimes your family too. Every time they see you, you are encouraging them to be the best of themselves and to love God as He has loved them. Since you have dedicated your life to service, they watch the way you practice what you preach. They become sponges by soaking up your stance, your communication style, your dress pattern, and even the way that you give. Why is it important to be "seen giving?" First, it is said that the senior minister of the church character is the one that most of the members take up because he is considered to be their spiritual leader. Knowing this, as the man of God, or appointed leader, your actions will begin to be duplicated by the members or even by those that have heard you speak. Whether you want this scrutiny or not, your life has become the example that the majority of the church will follow. Knowing this, if you don't give, the negative result doesn't just affect you, but it affects the whole congregation because ideally, you are the example. Make sure you understand that is necessary for people to see you giving. You are not giving because you want to be the center of attention, by you are giving so others recognize the importance of the task. Giving is an attribute of God, in fact, God's nature is to give. The Bible states in John 3:16; "For God so loved the world that He GAVE His only begotten Son, that whomsoever shall believe in Him shall not perish but have eternal life". Therefore, we must be as God and that is to give as we have prospered in our hearts, not grudgingly or of necessity, for God loves a cheerful giver (2 Corinthians 9:7). Our giving is the representation of how good God has been to us and how much we appreciate Him. As a leader in any capacity, are the people that you lead seeing you give your time, your talent, your treasure? Do you set the example that is needed so that your giving spirit can become contagious throughout your organization/ church? When you begin to develop a spirit of heartfelt giving and generosity, those that you lead will begin to immolate you in that capacity. Therefore, we must realize that as a leader or even a lay member it is important to follow the example of Matthew 5:16; "Let your light so shine before men, that they may see your good works, and glorify your Father which is in heaven". My grandfather always tried to be more of an example than a talker. He seemed to be the kind of example that allowed God to get the glory thereby through his actions people were saved and people stayed saved. So the bottom line is this, don't give to be seen, but you should be seen giving.

Meditation:

1 Corinthians 3:19-20 - For the wisdom of this world is foolishness with God. For it is written, He taketh the wise in their own craftiness.

_____

_____

_____

_____

_____

_____

Trust in the Lord

In any capacity of leadership, you will find yourself at some point wondering why you are serving in this role. Many times, it can seem as if people don't appreciate you and that your labor is done in vain. It is believed that many leaders are often overwhelmed by the continual pressure that comes their way on a daily basis which can eventually cause the leader to quit, or never seek leadership again. I have often felt these feeling that have been mentioned and sometimes life does get overwhelming, especially when God has given you a vision and those that you lead seem to push against it. Sometimes lack of funds or undesirable congregation can be discouraging to someone whom is attempting to lead people with vision. While growing up around my grandfather, he has always told me, "Trust in the Lord!" As a little kid growing up, I did not understand what that meant in its totality. I didn't believe that had anything in my life at the time that I had to "trust in the Lord" about. Therefore, I was oblivious to understanding the core meaning of this phrase. However, as I grew in age, I started to notice that life isn't always an easy journey specifically when people are following your leadership. At the age of 19 years old, I was given the reins to be the youth minister for my church and at that time we had quite a few young people attending the church. Here it is, I am at the age where I am still a teenager, but the way that I lived my life compelled the leadership to appoint me as youth minister. Although we had a decent number of youth, I immediately felt the pressure to meet a standard because of the position that I held. I was now the young man that had to make decisions about trips, encourage kids to do well in school, speak with parents about working alongside the youth, and building my communication skills to speak to older people about my position. I felt ready, but when I started the real work, I wasn't ready. Through all of my growth, I kept in my spirit, "trust in the Lord." Biblically, in Proverbs 3:5-6, it reads, "Trust in the Lord with all of your heart, and lean not to your own understanding, but in all of your ways acknowledge Him (God), and He will direct your paths". This scripture was anchored in my spirit. When I stared to get down, I leaned on it. When individuals came to me with problems, I leaned on it. When I didn't have anyone to talk to, I leaned on this scripture about trusting in the Lord. O young man, you must know that trials and tribulations are going to come but you must never lose faith or doubt because God is with you. As a leader, you are going to face adversities and even loneliness but if you have the Lord on your side, you will make it. After being youth minister for about ten years, I was told by my grandfather that he spoke to God and it was time for me to take the leadership of the church as the senior minister. At this time in my life, I was working for Florida Power and Light, I was single, and still trying to figure out what is it that God would have me do with my life. Interestingly, prior to my grandfather telling me this, I was staying with him in his home for about six months. I recall him sitting with me at night after dinner just pouring in me his wisdom, mistakes he made, disappointments, perspectives on life, and how to handle adversity. I did not know at the time, but he was preparing me for the work of church discipline, politics, and business. Through all of our conversations, he always said, "Trust in the Lord." As long as you trust in the Lord, meaning make Him your guide in all your decisions, you will make it. Therefore, it is my resolve that the Lord is able to strengthen me and sustain me as I do His Will, my duty will be to trust Him always in everything.

Meditation:

Colossians 2:8 - Beware lest any man spoil you through philosophy and vain deceit, after the tradition of men, after the rudiments of the world, and not after Christ.

_____

_____

_____

_____

_____

Always have money to get back

Church folk can sometimes be inconsiderate. Sometimes we can be the kind of people that will enjoy your giftedness from God, but don't see the benefit of blessing the vessel that God has used to display the gift. Many times we can devalue a person's worth based material things or who they surround themselves with. Therefore, if you have been called upon to display your gift, give your best to those that decide to listen to you or be attentive to your words. However, never assume that because a person has called you, they will bless you financially. Since this is the unfortunate reality, it is wise to always make sure you have enough money to get back home. As a preacher, people will call you for various reasons such as marital counseling, teaching a class, preaching a revival, facilitating a panel discussion, preaching at a funeral, or officiating a wedding. You may be called to exercise your gift from God, therefore, you must pray and communicate in a loving way what it is that helps you to do what you do. In order for the preacher to preach a funeral, he must cancel his appointments, put his clothes in the cleaners, take them out the cleaners, put gas in his car for the drive, get a haircut, make time for meditation of God's Word to come through him, possibly be the MC for the funeral, and be ready for bereavement counseling. Every funeral service that the preacher does, this person must be ready to do all these things because they have been "asked" to just preach the funeral. My grandfather would always remind me that we must never assume that when someone invites you to preach or give a lesson that they have counted the cost. Therefore, when you go to preach at a place, always make sure you have enough money to get back home. Do not depend on some of God's children because they will let you down. Some will act as if you are nobody and that being a minister is not a "professional" thing. I have had times where I was invited to a place and the congregation seemed excited to see me. They would even ask me if I needed anything before I deliver the word of God. However, at the end of the message, a baptism, and even a bottle of water, I was simply told, "have a blessed day." O man of God, you must know that people will sometimes not regard your worth and through your humility they may even try to conclude that you don't "expect" anything. Nevertheless, push forward and stay strong because God will bless you. Biblically, Apostle Paul in 2 Corinthians 11:8 – 10 states to the church in Corinth. "I robbed other churches, taking wages of them, to do you service. And when I was present with you, and wanted, I was chargeable to no man: for that which was lacking to me the brethren which came from Macedonia supplied: and in all things I have kept myself from being burdensome unto you, and so will I keep myself. As the truth of Christ is in me, no man shall stop me of this boasting in the regions of Achaia." (KJV) As Apostle Paul writes to this church, he simply tells them that they don't see his worth thereby they have not given him what is sufficient. He seems to tell those that are in the church at Corinth, "I gave you my time, talent, treasure but other churches compensated me for my time with you all." This wisdom will help you to be prepared for disappointments and even times of being letdown as you continue to minister to God's people.

Meditation:

Ecclesiastes 7:12 - For wisdom is a defense, and money is a defense: but the Excellency of knowledge [is, that] wisdom giveth life to them that have it.

_____

_____

_____

_____

_____

_____

Never counsel before you preach

As preachers, and/ or overseers it is without doubt that you want to help everybody. You know that people are hurting every day and they are in need of a Word from the Lord to make it in this world. This world is cruel and people often seem to care less about the problems of others. Therefore, people will seek out your advice, your counsel, and help because they believe you are able to guide them in the right direction. However, it won't be wise to counsel someone before you preach God's Word. Why? Often times throughout the week, God is speaking to the man of God through revelations and confirmations. God knows the problems that we are dealing with even before we bring them to the preacher. This section is not to stop the man of God from speaking to the congregation or being secluded, but it is to help the Holy Spirit to work throughout the congregation as he studies and meditates on God's Word. Mediating on the word before one preaches is valuable in so many ways. It is the thing that allows the Holy Spirit to reveal God's word to the man of God as he prepares to trigger a breakthrough and a transformation of God's people.

God desires to speak to his people, and he desires to guide them through the Word. My grandfather encouraged me to make sure that I am fully prepared to expound upon the word of God, and he believed this principle because he was occasionally accused of preaching on what someone had previously told him. At the time of my grandfather's tenure, he didn't have an office, nor did he have somewhere to meditate before he preaches God's word. Therefore, he often sat in Sunday school to focus on the lesson being taught while processing the message he would soon deliver in his spirit. Once he shared with me a situation that almost caused a few people to leave the congregation because they were under the impression that what they shared with him in confidence was public knowledge. To this day I do not know exactly what they shared with him, but his sermon that day was, "The Unruly Tongue." This sermon came from the book of James, and it included the points that we are to be submissive to the Spirit of God to tame the tongue. To learn how to speak second and hear first so that you do not speak evil of anyone or even make unfounded assumptions. From this message, they created the idea that he heard what they said and then decided to preach on "them" and not the word. As a result, my grandfather had to deal with accusations because assumptions were made. First, it is possible the answer to their question could have been in the sermon. Secondly, the assumption that his sermon was about their conversation would not have come up because he would not have had spoken with them before worship. As a senior minister of a church, I have learned to lean on this principle that seems to help me to encourage those that are hurting, and minister to those that need answers. Therefore, the thought is to try your best to meet with members in the weekday, after worship service if possible, but never before you preach. God knows what the people in your congregation needs and how they desire to be fed the word. People have problems, uncertainty, misconceptions, and doubts, but God has equipped you to preach the word both in season, and out of season. Satan will not triumph over the congregation for you have been given a fresh word for the people of God.

Meditation:

Proverbs 1:7 - The fear of the LORD [is] the beginning of knowledge: [but] fools despise wisdom and instruction.

_____

_____

_____

_____

_____

_____

Keep prayer in your life

Have you prayed today? Prayer can change things, and prayer gets the attention of God. It has always been a time of comfort for the weary and an opportunity to speak with your Father in heaven as you lay your burdens and cares to Him. I believe that in prayer we are given the opportunity to speak to God about the things on our heart. Therefore, as we approach His Majestic throne of Grace, we should come with thanksgiving in our hearts, and on our mind the power of God. The Bible speaks of 650 different type of prayers and countless amount of times we will see that prayer is mentioned in the Bible. Therefore, it seems like prayer is very important in the walk of the believer and in that walk they will develop solace. My grandfather continued to instill this idea in my spirit that I have to always stay prayerful to ensure I never lose my consistent communication with God. Being installed as a minister at the age of 28 years old at the same church that I grew up in was very overwhelming. It seemed to me that everyone was looking for me to fail, and it felt like the deck was stacked against me. However, during my first year of ministry, my grandfather continued to tell me to keep prayer in my life. In our nightly talks, he always told me that he had some struggles as being a minister for over thirty years, but prayer was the blessing that kept him spiritually aligned. As we live as Christians, we must always know that God has us in His Heart, and that He will always provide for us in the midst of a storm. As a minister, I find myself laying my burdens to the Lord, and He hears me. He always gives me the answers that I need to understand it better by and by. As a child of God, we must remember that prayer shows that our faith is in action and that we are giving our problems and offering thanksgiving unto God. Prayer is needed. It must be consistent in your life and it must be something you practice regularly. There will be many times in your life that you will have to press forward by faith because you may not know how things are going to work out in your favor, if you just keep the faith. Countless times we can track where many men and women trusted God through prayer and supplication. Prayer is defined as a solemn request for help or expression of thanks addressed to God or an object of worship. Therefore, we must always pray without ceasing, and be willing to be the kind of individuals that communicate to God daily.

Meditation:

Isaiah 11:2 - And the spirit of the LORD shall rest upon him, the spirit of wisdom and understanding, the spirit of counsel and might, the spirit of knowledge and of the fear of the LORD;

_____

_____

_____

_____

_____

_____

Stop playing and serve God

Have you ever had someone actually tell you, "stop playing!"? Well growing up I was told this by my grandfather a few times. Sometimes in life you may get distracted with the glory of the things that the world offers and not see that it is only temporary. Growing up, I was a good kid, if I may say so myself. I didn't get in too much trouble, but I did get in trouble occasionally. I recall a time when I was a teenager and my grandfather trusted me to accompany him to gospel meeting in Deerfield. My grandfather always tried to be on time for things, and he tried to be ready specifically if I was supposed to be picking him up. He reminded me throughout the week that we are scheduled to attend this gospel meeting and that he was depending on me to pick him up. However, earlier the day if the gospel meeting, a friend invited me to play basketball. As the time for the gospel meeting drew near, I made a detour and began playing basketball with my friend(s) and totally forgot about this gospel meeting. As the time continued to get closer, my cell phone kept ringing and I didn't hear it, nor had it near me because

I was playing basketball. When the game was concluded, I walked over to my cell phone and saw that I had three missed calls from my grandfather. It was at that time I remembered I was supposed to pick him up so that we could go to the gospel meeting. I immediately ran to my car and drove out of the parking lot as if I was a raging maniac. In the process of me driving, I called my grandfather, and in the most humble voice he could have, he said, "I am waiting on you", and it was at that time I felt so bad because he didn't yell, he simply said, "I am waiting on you." By the grace of God, I made it to pick him up, and we made it to that gospel meeting and had great fellowship. As a result of this, I began to tell myself that I had to become more serious about my responsibilities and the work of God. Many times we get caught up in the midst of trying to fit in, becoming popular, or even trying to be like everyone else. However, God desires for us to be peculiar people, a chosen generation (1 Peter 2:9), which means that we must never strive to be like the world and the sin in it. As a young man I realize that in order to be the person that God called me to be, I must be willing to be different. Therefore, I strove to take advantage of every opportunity that I had to be exposed to knowledge and wisdom that would make me mentally stronger. As a result, I was able to avoid some pitfalls that were sure to come.

Meditation:

*James 1:5 - **If any of you lack wisdom, let him ask of God, that giveth to all [men] liberally, and upbraideth not; and it shall be given him.***

_____

_____

_____

_____

_____

_____

Two people arguing will never solve anything

As a leader you will find yourself sometimes getting frustrated with the people that you lead and sometimes things may not go the way you hoped. Therefore, we must be encouraged to know that although we disagree, let us not be disagreeable. My grandfather once told me this very wisdom principle after a very interesting day at the church building. One day at the church building there was a woman after worship that waited for him to finish shaking hands and speaking to visitors. Once he completed that, she began to yell, "Bro. Holt, I have an issue about one of your church members!" As she yelled, he calmly said, "How can I help you my sister?" As she continued to yell this, he continued to be calm and continued to remain with a peaceful demeanor in spite of her aggression. Once they began to speak, she stated that she had an issue with one of the brothers in the church and she stated how she had been doing things with him that wasn't becoming of a child of God. As she spoke at a vocal level that seemed to be higher than it should be considering she was a few feet away, he spoke in a tone of understanding. During their dialogue, she continued to accuse this guy of being a hypocrite, and it seemed like she was saying it was the minister's fault. As I listened from afar, my grandfather listened and offered advice that seemed to calm her down and allow her to begin to reexamine her approach. This guidance seemed to help her to think clearly. Although I did not know everything that was said during this conversation, I saw my grandfather use this wisdom point to calm down a person that seemed to be ready for verbal combat and a possible physical altercation. After he spoke with this woman and I was taking him home after evening worship, I asked him how he was able to calm this person down. He stated so humbly, "two people arguing will never solve anything" and he began to explain what he said to her, and more importantly how he said it to her. It is important to know that we should never go into a conversation ready to argue, especially if we are expected to be to be the leader. Furthermore, when you allow a person that is driven by anger to control the conversation, you will not be able to come to a resolve that is not driven by emotions. You must strive to hold your emotions together and allow your mind to be clear of biases and/ or subjective opinion. In your company, family, congregation, and/ or your personal business, you must understand that when you are involved in a conflict it can cause you to lose control, and thereby make you out of control. As we strive to be better leaders and individuals we must know that God desires for us to be stronger men and women and never allow ourselves to be in a place of anger and wrath. God will help you find the answers and He will guide your mind to deal with the situation with love and peace.

Meditation:

Proverbs 12:28 - "Even a fool, when he holdeth his peace, is counted wise: and he that shutteth his lips is esteemed a man of understanding."

Keep money in your pocket

My grandmother, a strong, loving, and spiritual lady told me that I can make it in this world if I just keep God first. Throughout out my life she always encouraged me especially during times when I wanted to give up. One day I was at her house and she asked me to go to the store and purchase something for her. However, I didn't have any money in my pocket, nor was I able to access it at the time of her request. She stated to me that I should always have money in my pocket because you never know when I will encounter an emergency. My grandmother, a.k.a. Big Mama, who was the mother of eight children and grandmother of many grandchildren, was a woman of elegance and inner strength. My grandmother, Helen S. Holt, was the person I spoke with when I felt down and I wasn't sure to whom I could confide. She was such a great listener. She always gave advice that would carry you through your trials and troubles that were going on in your life. Her smile lit up the room, and her speech was that of a queen sitting on her royal horse. She told me this wisdom principle with the underlying thought of always be prepared and be ready to handle adversity. It is not always in many people's interest to carry cash because we live in a world of technology and online purchasing. Therefore, cash seems to be an anomaly and many people never use it anymore. To be ready as a leader means you need to be ready to make a purchase on the side of the road or when you must make a purchase right away while the deal is hot. My grandmother's advice gave me this wisdom and it has helped me to be a better leader.

Meditation:

Proverbs 22:7 - "The rich rules over the poor, and the borrower becomes the lender's slave."

_____

_____

_____

_____

_____

_____

Always learn everything you can about your job

In the year 2001 I applied for my first job after graduating from high school. It is without a doubt that I wasn't sure what my steps in life were going to be, but one thing I knew was that I needed to get a job or go to school. After a few weeks of putting in applications, I received a call for an interview from Kentucky Fried Chicken regarding the cook position. After being interviewed for the position, I was hired to work thirty hours a week starting that next week. During my excitement about finally having my first job, I spoke with my grandfather about how I couldn't wait to begin to make my own money and not have to ask my mother/ father for any more money (still trying to do that). During our conversation, my grandfather stated that he was very proud of me and that he has been praying for me in this manner. Furthermore, he discussed with me how I should make sure that I give to God the first ten percent of my paycheck and budget the remaining. In addition, he gave me the advice to learn all that I can about the job and the company so that I could be ready to fill a slot when it becomes vacant. Once I started working at Kentucky Fried Chicken, I began as a cook with the responsibilities of cleaning the frozen chicken, loading/ unloading, preparing side orders, and keeping the kitchen clean. During this time of being a cook, I took my grandfather's advice and learned all that I could about the position and occasionally watched how other positions functioned. After being a cook for five months, I was asked if I wanted to try out the cashier position because of them being shorthanded. Immediately, I said, "sure" because I was ready to fill it because I had already prepared myself for the challenge. Therefore, I was given the position because I was ready, and the opportunity presented itself creating a chance for me to succeed. Now I am a multi-position employee with the ability to be a cook and/ or a cashier on any given day. As a result of me being prepared and heeding my grandfather's advice, I was now on the schedule more and I began to understand how to better service each customer knowing what it took to get them their meal. After working in both roles for a few months, I was offered the shift supervisor position for the morning shift which I was honored to accept. At the age of 19 years old, I was able to be a cook, cashier, and now a shift supervisor overseeing a group of teammates that are older than me. It is important to know that in any sector of your life whether business, personal, church, or even corporate you must always try to aspire to be the best that you can be. Moving forward, while I was working at this Kentucky Fried Chicken, I noticed that the more responsibility that I obtained, the more issues I had to deal with. You must always strive to be better than the average. As I allowed this wisdom to be in my spirit, I approach every job that I had since Kentucky Fried Chicken in the same manner. As a result, I have been promoted countless times, I have received many raises in pay, and I've been able to be a better leader by the grace of God. It is without a doubt that I truly appreciate the advice my grandfather gave me, and I am thankful for his wisdom because of it, I always stay hungry for more.

Meditation:

Ecclesiastes 7:1 - "For the protection of wisdom is like the protection of money, and the advantage of knowledge is that wisdom preserves the life of him who has it."

_____

_____

_____

_____

_____

_____

Expose your children to the world

As a young man I have traveled to many places. I haven't been all over the world, but I have seen a lot of things that many children that were my age didn't see. Growing up, my family always traveled and they attended countless family reunions throughout the country. I have been to Canada, Mississippi, California, Alabama, Georgia, Texas, all parts of Florida, and New Mexico. Although this is not everywhere in the world, it allowed me to be exposed to many different schools of thought and exposed to many types of people. It is important to expose your children to the world and to allow them to see more than just the neighborhood that they live in. By visiting these various cities, I learned that all black people aren't thugs, all mothers are not single mothers, and all jobs are not offered in restaurants. The opportunity to visit these places and see how things were in these cities exposed me so that I was less likely to conform to some of the behaviors and attitudes prevalent in Miami. I remember I was speaking with my friend and I asked him had he ever been to Orlando and he remarked that he had never been out of Overtown, which is a small city in Miami, Fl. Later that night I spoke with my mother and she revealed to me that we as her children were blessed and quite fortunate whereas other children may not be. We as a people must expose our children to the things in the world such as library trips, art museums, football games, amusement parks, Wall Street, conferences, and places that allow them to see greater than where they currently are. My mother showed me the world by allowing me to go on field trips and out of town trips with my sports teams. As a result, I find myself not being content with certain things because I know that things are better and can be better. However, I realize the Bible is correct in Hosea 4:6; "My people are destroyed for lack knowledge: because thou hast rejected knowledge…" In the context of this scripture it speaks about irresponsible priests, but in practical application it speaks to the fact that knowledge is power. Many times our children are robbed of the ability to see things that will be helpful to them and allow them to see that success does exist beyond their present circumstances. As a young man, my grandfather showed me that I can be great and he allowed me to see the greatness of preachers, attorneys, teachers, fathers, engineers, and even janitors. He always made a point to put me in the room of people that had achieved greatness so that I can aspire to be greater as a young man. As a result, I am still aspiring to be great and to achieve greater because I know that greater exist.

My encouragement is that we expose our young girls and boys to the world so that they can be better so that they can be stronger. Take them to the moon and back so that they will know how it feels to soar.

Meditation:

Proverbs 15:24 - "The path of life leads upward for the wise to keep him from going down to the grave."

_____

_____

_____

_____

_____

_____

Prayer Changes things!

Have you prayed today? Prayer is an essential part of maintaining your relationship with God, and trusting in His Word. Therefore, as you lead, you should always pray. As you prepare to make a decision, pray. As you are attempting to try something different, pray. The Bible reminds us in Philippians 4: 6-7; Do not be anxious about anything, but in every situation, by prayer and petition, with thanksgiving, present your requests to God. And the peace of God, which transcends all understanding, will guard your hearts and your minds in Christ Jesus. It is without a doubt that God desires to hear from His children which shows their faith in Him. I have learned that prayer is essential to growing in the Lord, and that personally it has been a strong part of me growing up. I recall as a little kid, being encouraged to pray before you partake of any meal. Like most children that have grown up in any type of religious home, they know the famous prayer that was taught. I remember my mother teaching me to say, "God is great, and God is good, and we thank

Him for our food, bow our heads we must be feed, give us Lord our daily bread…Amen." This prayer was oftentimes recited every time we came together, specifically with the children. Although the prayer seems quick, it is precise in its message as giving honor to God for His provision. Throughout the Bible, prayer is the driving force of many faith warriors, and they believed that God answers prayers. My grandfather, like many Christians believed in prayer, and knew that God was going to show His power when His faithful children call upon His Holy Name. For example, we had an issue at the church building where finances were low, and it seemed like the church was in the valley of despair. The members were not giving as they normally would, and some of the great givers passed away. Knowing this, my grandfather started to lean upon Matthew 7:7; "Ask, and it will be given you; seek and you will find; knock, and the door will be opened to you." This scripture was the one that he recited as the church went through this difficult time, and he began to fast and pray. There were a few times when I was with him that he told me about the church's problem, but he ended by saying, "I am praying about it." At the age of twelve, I wasn't sure the totality of what he was saying but I did understand that he was talking to God about it. Many time we go through difficulties in our lives which seem to be overwhelming because we don't know how everything will end. Nevertheless, we must never stop talking to God, or seeking His face in the problem that we may be dealing with. Furthermore, we must always strive to let God know our cares, our burdens, our feelings because quite frankly, HE CARES! The Bible reminds us in 1 Peter 5:7; "Casting all your care upon Him, because He cares for you." God cares for you, and He knows what you are going through but He is waiting for you to seek His face in the midst of your circumstance. My grandfather prayed about the church issue that was mentioned earlier, and by the power of God, everything worked out. The church continued to be faithful to God's word, and began to see how God opened up doors that seemed to be shut close. We must never forget to pray or seek God in our troubles. The proverb writer says in Proverbs 3:5-6; "Trust in the LORD with all thine heart; and lean not unto thine own understanding. In all thy ways acknowledge him, and he shall direct thy paths." Always pray, and remember to never lose hope for God is going to make a way somehow!

Meditation:

Colossians 2:2 - "My goal is that they may be encouraged in heart and united in love, so that they may have the full riches of complete understanding, in order that they may know the mystery of God, namely, Christ."

_____

_____

_____

_____

_____

_____

Sometimes you have to walk alone

I've never been a very sociable person, nor have I ever been a person that enjoys speaking in public. However, I find myself in a place where I have to give advice and speak in front of hundreds of people often. Therefore, I cannot afford to be shy because I am depended upon by too many people and they need my encouragement to make it through the "storms" in their lives. However, I have had to recognize that through the storms of life, I must not allow others problems to be my problems. I must not allow someone else's pain to cause me to loss my mind knowing that God is in control. Therefore, sometimes you have to learn to walk alone. This wisdom is not a principle that means you have to be a loner or someone that is not friendly but you must learn that alone time is needed. Growing up in a big family we spent a lot of time together for birthdays and even funerals. My family loved to get together and we enjoyed each other so much that sometimes we saw each other every day. It was difficult to be alone or to have quiet time because in my family when you desire to be alone, they assume that something is wrong with you or something has happened to you. The reason they were this way was because we all loved each other, and we are very concerned about each other's well-being. I truly love my family, and I am so thankful for them and their support. However, I recognized that through all of the commotion and family time, my grandfather found time in the peak of the night to be alone. He often times set at his dining room table to read the Bible, listen to Bible tapes, or even write down his sermon notes. This particular thing amazed me, and it caused me to begin to emulate this same practice. As a young boy beginning to preach sermonettes, I studied at the peak of the night, and I gathered my thoughts while everyone was sleeping. There was something about alone time that allowed God to speak to my spirit and for me to hear His voice regarding His Word. It seemed like God spoke to me in my quiet times and that He gave me the answers to my questions as I walked alone. My friend, you must realize that too many people around you can sometimes block you from hearing God's voice. Furthermore, having the wrong people around you restricts your ability to make proper self-examination that could be vital towards your growth and development. Sometimes you have to walk alone so that you will be able to stay away from harm's way that comes with many people around you. Someone once said, "You could do badly all by yourself", so if I desire to be in trouble then I will be in trouble alone. I have learned that when you walk with God, sometime people will even detach themselves from you because of your walk with Him thereby causing you to walk alone. My grandfather didn't seek attention, nor did he yearn for it. Growing up as a child and then young man I only remember him being with his family and his close preaching friends. His circle wasn't big, but it was powerful and spiritual. Whenever he allowed me to drive him to a gospel meeting, conference, or a church function it was just the two of us. Biblically, we find countless time where the child of God walked with the Lord and how God spoke to the prophets directly meaning they were alone with God. As you go throughout your life, you must remember that there is no shame in detaching, going solo or even being alone because you may find more happiness alone than with many friends.

Meditation:

Colossians 4:5-6 - "Be wise in the way you act toward outsiders; make the most of every opportunity. Let your conversation be always full of grace, seasoned with salt, so that you may know how to answer everyone."

_____

_____

_____

_____

_____

_____

Get Some Rest

The senior shepherd of any organization works hard, and he/ she deserves to have a vacation or even a sabbatical from the daily functions that can become overwhelming. Leading a group of people to accomplish a united goal is tough, and if you are not careful, you will end up losing your strength to lead them effectively. People come with many personalities and attitudes because we all have an opinion and in some cases we all think that we are "right". Therefore, as the leader, you must learn how to get some rest because you cannot lead effectively if you don't have good health, or tired all the time. This principle is something that I find myself continually working on because no manner how much you do, it always more things to do within your organization. By the time I began preaching and really comprehending what my grandfather was doing, he had retired from FEC railroad and was basically being a senior minister full-time. In our conversation, he shared with me this principle as he began to enter his old age. My grandfather physically was strong as an ox, and was able to move around as he desired without any serious assistance. I recall when we as a church was doing evangelism work in the community, and as he went door to door encouraging people to come to worship, he kept saying that his stomach wouldn't stop hurting. Nevertheless, he pushed through the pain, and completed that task. Later on that night, he still was complaining about the pain in his stomach but he took some medicine and went to bed in spite of the pain. After worship that next morning, someone was able to encourage my grandfather to go to the hospital and get himself checked out, and thank God he listened. Later on the afternoon, we received a call that my grandfather appendix had busted a few days ago, and that he was "lucky" to be alive. The appendix sits at the junction of the small intestine and large intestine. According to webmd.com, the appendix acts as a storehouse for good bacteria, "rebooting" the digestive system after diarrheal illness. Furthermore, the appendix if ruptured causes severe pain in the right lower part of the belly. Along with nausea and vomiting. My grandfather was littering walking around with bacteria uncontrolled in his body. As he was at the hospital, he had to undergo a surgery to heal what had busted. As a leader, we can work long hours, neglect quality family time, and even sacrifice our own health for the good of the company, and still not complete every task. The bottom line is that you need to take time out to rest, and to enjoy the one life the God has given you before it passes you by. My grandfather spoke to me a few times as he was in the latter years of his leadership at Brownsville church of Christ, and he told me to make sure I take time to rest my body, my mind, and spend quality time with my family. After the healing of my grandfather's appendix, he seemed to not allow the stress of ministry get him burdened down. Of course there was a lot of work to be done, but he realized that he couldn't do everything himself. According to a study done by inthyword.org in 2005 and 2006, one thousand fifty (1,050 or 100%) pastors we surveyed, every one of them had a close associate or seminary buddy who had left the ministry because of burnout, conflict in their church, or from a moral failure. We, as pastors, leaders, minsters all have been blessed with a calling to lead the people of God as the leave on this earth. Quiet as it is kept, some people act as if they don't want to be led to the goal of being Christ – like, therefore, as the leader you must come to the resolve that all you can do is your best. Another shocking stat according to inthyword.org, nine hundred thirty-five, (935 or 89%) of the pastors we surveyed also considered leaving the ministry at one time. Five hundred ninety, (590 or 57%) said they would leave if they had a better place to go-including secular work. The work of a man of God is overwhelming, but you must remember that you cannot help others if you are not well, or getting the proper rest. A few days ago, my family and I flew to New York for a family reunion, and the presentation that is presented on the airplane says that in the case of an emergency, put your mask on first before you can help out anyone with their mask. Simply put, get some rest, and pray to God to give you the strength to endure until the end. O young man of God, you can't do it all, but whatever you do, do your best.

Meditation:

Psalm 127: 2 - "It is vain for you to rise up early, To retire late, To eat the bread of painful labors; For He gives to His beloved even in his sleep."

_____

_____

_____

_____

_____

_____

Teach Change, Don't Force Change

The vision that has been given to you by God at times can be so overwhelming that it creates a sense of urgency in your spirit. You have within your mind where things should be, but somehow, but reality has not aligned with what's inside your mind, therefore, we must be patient. Rosa Beth Moss Kanter states, "A vision is not just a picture of what could be; it is an appeal to our better selves, a call to become something more." Whenever we see that something can be more, be better, and efficient to many leaders it make sense to change. However, if you change without teaching who, what, when, where, how or why, we can end up in a land along without help. My grandfather told me this wisdom as I became minster of the church with the aim of trying to guide my eagerness to get things done right away. He spoke with me every day telling me to preach the Word, and allow that to prick the hearts of the people. As a young minister, I watched for countless of years of the ups and downs of the church and in my mind I always said, "If I was the leader of this, I bet they would listen to me." It was the mentality that individuals on the outside get that are looking in and making critics about how they can do a better job. As I began to enter into this calling from God to minister to His children, I quickly learned that you cannot force change. I recall in my first year, I wanted to start a mentorship program for older men to teach the younger men. In my mind I saw the older men excited about the idea to assist with the training of our young men and assisting with their development. In my mind I saw the younger men so thrilled to learn from the older men in the church that have been through the trials and tribulations in life, but they made it through. I felt like a civil rights leader that stated, "I have a dream!" Therefore, on one Sunday I asked all the men and young men to stay in after worship, so that I can speak with them about this new ministry that we are going to start next month. As I spoke to the men and young men, I told them that starting next week, we will have a list of the adult men, and the young men and I was going to pair them with each other, and I expect all the men to participate because God has given me this vision for the church. After I discussed the importance of such a ministry, and slightly demanded they be a part of it, we prayed and everyone went their separate ways. When next month arrived after having the sign-up sheet on the bulletin board for a month, only three men signed their names out of twenty men. It was at that time I realized that I had attempted to force change and not teach it. Since that was the case, I realized that these men did not "buy in" to what I was explaining, they heard what I said, but they weren't taught on why they should. I tried for a few weeks to push this mentorship program, but it didn't work in which the way that I anticipated it to work. I realized what my grandfather told me was right, which was to not force change. So many times we desire to have things done our way, which may be better but we have to make sure that those we are depending on to carry out the vision understand it clearly. Lastly, we must recognize that change can only happen when a person is uncomfortable, and recognize that change is needed in order for the thing to flourish.

Meditation:

Isaiah 28: 29 – "All this also comes from the Lord Almighty, whose plan is wonderful, whose wisdom is magnificent."

Be Yourself

Growing up I have had the opportunity to travel across the United States at the expense of my grandfather to lectureships, revivals, gospel meetings, and various congregations. Our travels were very eye-opening for me because I was able to meet the top echelon of preachers in the churches of Christ. As I sat and listened to them, and many others time and time again, I noticed that many men had styles in their deliveries of preaching that truly was engaging and came with clarity. However, often times I noticed that many men emulated one another which in essence made sense, but it took away from their originality. My grandfather discussed with me many times to strive to be myself, and use the talent that God gave me while enhancing it through scholastic study. He stated that God has anointed you to be a unique carrier of His Word, and He will guide you by His Spirit as you deliver His Word. It is your uniqueness that makes you special, and by being unique in your craft, God will get all the credit in your elevation. Therefore, as I grew up, I always strived to be different, and to not be conformed to the styles of my brothers or sisters in their delivery or presentation of God's word. Of course, I have taken a little sound bite here, and a little sound bite there, but I have always attempted to add my personality to it and not simply trying to duplicate the person that gave it. It is important to be yourself because that is what God has designed you to be, and he desires for you to use the gift that is inside of you, and not another's gift. Paul in Ephesians 2:10 states, "For we are his workmanship, created in Christ Jesus for good works, which God prepared beforehand, that we should walk in them." We are created specifically for the purpose of God, and He has designed us for good works which will allow Him to get the glory and honor, and all the praise. God has made you beforehand to be special, and He desires for you to show the world how much your talents and gifts that are meant to bless them in a mighty way. You must be yourself, and allow your light to shine, your face to smile, and for your head to be held high because you are fearfully, wonderfully made. In my opinion, my grandfather was very unique, and his attitude was such that he understood that life was easier when you be yourself regardless of the shift of society. My goal in this book is to encourage leaders, teachers, ministers, business executives, and our youth to know that we must always keep pressing on for the prize that God has laid hold of me. My grandfather poured into me knowledge that is everlasting, and he always inspired me to be myself, and keep God first in everything that I do. The first thing you must know in regards to being yourself is that you are the best person that can be you, and no one can do you, like you. Growing up I remember when many young men wanted to be like a certain NBA hall of famer. Throughout his career he was widely considered to be the greatest basketball player to ever live, and in some circles he still is the greatest. While I was in my teens, many boys and men shaved their head just to be like this player. It was so amazing that a man could have such an influence on a society that he effected the way many measured themselves. For example, if this famous basketball player started to grow a beard, many of the people that were his fans started to do the same thing. If this famous basketball player wore his shorts very high while he played basketball, his fans would do the same thing. Sometimes we are so influenced by the things we see our heroes, movie stars, or even favorite leaders that we lose our identity because we are trying so hard to be like them. If you could define yourself, how would that look? It should be your goal to be unique, and to create your lane with your personality, and the ability that God has possessed you with. Today you have the opportunity to show the world whom you really are, and I encourage you to do that. This world needs you to be yourself, we have too many imitators, and duplicators. Be yourself, and always strive to let your uniqueness shine!

Meditation:

Exodus 18: 17 – 19 – "Moses' father-in-law replied, "What you are doing is not good. You and these people who come to you will only wear yourselves out. The work is too heavy for you; you cannot handle it alone. Listen now to me and I will give you some advice, and may God be with you. You must be the people's representative before God and bring their disputes to him."

_____

_____

_____

_____

_____

_____

__MAY THE WORDS OF MY MOUTH AND THE MEDITATION OF MY HEART BE ACCEPTABLE IN THE LORD'S SIGHT, WHOM IS MY STRENGTH AND MY REDEEMER__

www.ingramcontent.com/pod-product-compliance
Lightning Source LLC
LaVergne TN
LVHW041545070426
835507LV00011B/937